markings on earth

native writers' circle of the americas/wordcraft circle

first book awards

EVELINA ZUNI LUCERO, *night sky, morning star*

JANET McADAMS, *the island of lost luggage*

KARENNE WOOD, *markings on earth*

series editor, geary hobson

markings on earth

karenne wood

the university of arizona press   tucson

The University of Arizona Press
First printing
∞ This book is printed on acid-free, archival-quality paper.
Manufactured in the United States of America
06   05   04   03   02   01   6   5   4   3   2   1

Library of Congress Cataloging-in-Publication Data
Wood, Karenne, 1960–
Markings on earth / Karenne Wood.
p. cm. – (First book awards)
ISBN 0-8165-2165-4 (pbk. : alk.paper)
1. Monacan Indians–Poetry.   2. Virginia–Poetry.
I. Title. II. Series
PS3623.063 M37 2001
811´.6–dc21
2001001178

British Library Cataloguing-in-Publication Data
A catalogue record for this book is available from the British Library.

Publication of this book is made possible in part by the proceeds of a
permanent endowment created with the assistance of a Challenge Grant
from the National Endowment for the Humanities, a federal agency.

For my family and my people

Everything is a prayer for this journey.
—Joy Harjo

contents

markings on earth

Directions

I.

East is a genesis, *house made of
dawn*, where streaked clouds in
lavender, red, orange brush the
world's edge, where the dance
circle begins. Doors of domed
wigwams face morning. From
pipestone, tobacco smoke wafts
as striated light washes rivers
with green. Deep in the forest,
fiddleheads unfold. Green of new
leaf: the bright glossy hair rises
through red clay, lighting the world.

II.

South is the summer's white heat
without shade. Yellowing grasses
bend with wind's breath as bulrushes
lean over bodies of lovers, clothes
peeled like fruit skins, the limp
sleeves of August forgotten.
Hydrangeas blossom in blues,
whites, beyond tongues of tiger
lily's flames. Among bee balm,
hummingbirds hover. Every
live thing grows, sinking roots
deeper into the black rock.

III.

West is a space of thought, sparse
land with cliffs brushed magenta
and gold. Leaves slowly turn
to sunset hues as women gather

chokeberries, the elder men
crafting gourd rattles, singing
thin clouds into lightning for
corn. We, who cannot stay here
forever, read the cliff's face
where our ancestors wrote to us,
pictures in ocher. Beyond a vast
darkness, they wait for us.

IV.

North is the country of reflected light.
Shadows like wolves: the curved fang
takes moose by its haunches, spatters
scarlet fire onto ice. Footprints
recede into tundra. Aurora borealis —
a dance among spirits — new snow
piled on boughs, ribs gnawed with
scrimshawed grooves. Death groans
startle horizons, grow still. Bones
trace edges of ptarmigan, caribou.
White-out: a porcelain bear waits
beside the world's ice-crusted rim.

V.

Sky is the casing of our breath,
suspending stars. The azimuth's
violet arc sends snow, gently,
and hurtles bright flashes like war
cries through darkness. Lightning
bugs zigzag above us, tiny
phosphorescent lamps. Celestial
palette: turquoise, cerulean, cobalt,
azure. Among its luminaries,
the sun walks the world's edge.

A brilliant moon rises while bats
leave caverns for air, another home.

VI.

What to say about the earth, whose
love lives like bright knives within us?
Like us, it is alchemy: chromium,
zinc, magnesium, copper. Like us,
a fire swirls within. Disordered,
too, the balanced skewed. The
stones, the trees, the waters speak.
And if we are dust, as earth is,
let it receive us into the embrace
we barely left, memory remembered,
green as young bones: O, let the
next world look just like this one.

VII.

This is a prayer, its palms
already curved around our dust.
Lovers sing out from grasses they
become, sing to us: Here. Now.
This ground. These mountains,
skirted in mist. This hallowed
distance between worlds, where
sage, sweetgrass, and cedar burn,
the smoke intertwined with your
hair. We who have loved you
grow as dark roots beneath your
toes. We touch you. Here. Now.

blue mountains

Blue Mountains

Bury me up there in the high blue mountains
and I promise that I will return to teach the wind
how to make poetry from tossed about and restless leaves.
—*Lorna Goodison*

Beyond Charlottesville, mountains lift ridges toward
clouds, cropped where towers or ski slopes are rising.
The land undulates

in paintspots of redbud, azalea, columbine,
dogwood, apple blossom, then pine and cedar, surprising
chartreuse of new hay that, come autumn, will sit
spiral-rolled in the fields, steam wavering upward
as though it could breathe —

past white-fenced
pastures in Albemarle, each claimed by someone
the ground will eventually own.

Sometimes, enveloped in fog,
we become almost spirit, lifted away — we think
this is like wanting to die — and wrench ourselves back
to breathe our way hard into Amherst, home country.

Drive down, up Father Judge Road, where Bear Mountain
leans from Tobacco Row, a row of blue mountains we never
abandoned and lavender mist that swathes High Peak
the way old women's shawls wrap around their knees.

Now a thin glint of light flashes, tears of one or another
who still weeps for us and the ever-loving earth. The mountains
speak in our voices:

this too will pass,
this, and this. We, who remain, also will pass

into their realm,
                    restless as leaves, to shine
beneath feet of contemporary Pilgrims, tearing
at surfaces, skittering across the earth's face.

We have nothing to teach the wind nuzzling itself
across the land, its poetry beyond mortal language.
Bury us in the blue mountains, our bodies
the earth they have always been.
                              We will grow
into trees and animals, turn soil back to elk's grass
and ask to return as an elemental brightness
that gleams with the most furious love.

Great Blue Herons

They swoop from overhead, pterodactyls
or gliders, trailing legs. How to perform
the seamless arc, sky to water, we wonder,
peering through green camouflage.
We can identify, describe with tapered
words that should fly, themselves, like
aerodyne or *avatar*, and never know the long
glide with legs reaching earthward to leave
eight-inch tracks in the sand. These birds
do not love us nor wish to know us better —
they fly with awkward take-offs as we approach,
then land beyond us, made of elegance and air,
to stand where the swollen Rappahannock roils,
swirling over boulders, and silver shad flash
toward waters of their origins. The migration
cocks the herons into motionless poses like
statues of birds, each hunter's eye fixed just
below the surface. Rooted to the bank, we watch
the hunt with similar eyes. We were never so still.

Spider Dance

Upside-down,
suspended on the ribs of her rigging,
she is regal in black and gold velvet.
At web's edge,
unmoving, her suitor waits.

Two days he remains,
smaller than the female,
mostly legs and inflated sex organ
whose clear tendril unfurls like a fern.

He crawls cautiously,
as though he knows (does he know?)
that she may devour him —
she has bitten off one of his legs.
His craving compels him
to enter the warm, liquid womb
where her poisons are conjured.

His sex, hard as glass now, propels itself on
toward her softer parts, restless eggs,
floating. When she turns upon him,
he does not leap to safety but is taken
within her completely and dies
at the exact moment some of us wish to die.

Encased in a sac she weaves
before the killing frost,
tiny spiders will emerge, parachute
on spring's breath, to repeat
her quiet strategy, his need.

The Raccoon

We fished afternoon's haze on the river awhile,
hoped for stripers but caught a few perch and two
channel cats; then we heard a cry unlike any we knew,
its harsh *chit chit chit chit* and *kriiiee   kriiiee*
a nasal, raptorial utterance, over and over, until
we stared toward shore. On the beach a raccoon
leapt toward a fallen tree into the water, doused
something held in its paws, leapt ashore, quieted,
screeched again, twisting and springing. Ten minutes
passed as we speculated: blue crabs perhaps, their
ridged pincers sunk in raccoon flesh — still the continuous
wauling and wauling, dousing and silence again. A heron
swept down a distance away and watched too. Another
five minutes. The raccoon shook its head, lumbering off.
We checked our lines, cast again — something crawled
out of the water. *What was it?* small, certainly
wet: we could not see. We coughed the boat's engine
alive, veered it over, to find you, young raccoon,
bedraggled, bitten, perched on a stump. You were
blind, almost killed, and by one of your own. We could
not know whether it was your mother who wanted
to drown you, or a territorial male, or one perhaps rabid,
whether some of those screeches were yours, whether
you were blinded at birth or just now had clamped your
eyes tight at the horror of it all. You survived with your
limp, ringed tail, your sorry fur, your mask in which
no lights were shining, and as we turned the boat
toward our own shore because we have learned
about endings and knew yours already, and because
we could not change it, you flung your arms through
the indifferent air like one of us recently born, arms

attached to miniature hands — you uttered a small cry,
or you didn't — you turned your face with its useless
slits for eyes upward and asked a dark world for your life.

Celebrating Corn

Pounding the pestle
against a white stone,
she grinds last year's kernels to meal.
                    I have planted my corn

A thin white-gold powder
clings to her hands.
Around her, air shimmers.
                    I have planted it with my song

One of the puppies is barking,
staccato *yap yap*
punctuating her strokes.
                    Let it grow tall and beautiful

Beside her, an aunt stitches
shell beads to deerskin, as young women
lean toward clay pots, stirring embers.
                    washed in sunlight

The men are out gathering
red clay for ocher. Beyond domed
bark houses, fields
                    watered by rains

stretch small earthen mounds
toward the river. Redbuds blossom,
their branches upturned like hands.
                    Grandmother, we plant our seeds

She pats meal into ashcakes. Already
night falls as a smell of bread rises.
Painted, the men drum their song.
celebrating corn.

Amoroleck's Words

You can't take a man's words.
They are his even as the land
is taken away
where another man
builds his house.
    —Linda Hogan

You must've been a sight, Captain John Smith,
as your dugout approached
with Jamestown's men
sporting plumed hats,
poufed knickers, beards, stockings,
funny little shoes.
You might have looked, to us,
well,
uncivilized.
We fought you, we know,
because you wrote it down.
One man was left behind. Wounded.
At your mercy. Among your shining goods —
mirrors, knives, firearms, glass beads —
where was mercy? Maybe you left it
in England. Eager to learn, Captain Smith,
you asked about the worlds he knew,
whether there was gold,
why his people had fought
when you came to them "in love."
He told you in his dialect,
which no one now speaks.
You recorded his name. His words.
Not his fate.
Of all the words our people spoke

in the year of your Lord 1608,
only his answer remains:
"We heard that you were a people
come from under the world,
to take our world from us."

Chief Totopotamoi, 1654

after Miller Williams

This is to say we continued. As though continuing changed us.
As though continuing brought happiness as we had known.

On a dry field without cover, his skin blistered raw in the sun.
Not one among us came, as though he had no relations.

What did we say to our brother? How could we leave him alone
while soldiers guarded his corpse as though precious to them?

One of the women, in darkness, crept to the field where he died,
prayed for him, covered him up. Dust over what was not dust.

We would have ventured out with her if we had loved ourselves less.
We had to think of our children, and he was not coming back.

How could we live with the silence, live with our grief and our shame?
Death did not heal what he suffered. He was making demands.

We did not want him to be there, asking the question he asked us,
changing the sound of his name. He had embarrassed us.

This is the memory we carried, avoiding the thought that he remained
face down among the charred grasses, holding the earth with his hands.

Site of a Massacre

Can you say you see
only a field or hear
nothing but breeze
where the earth raises
grass now, the wind,
then the barefoot dead run
before a gunstock crashed
into her skull, thuds of
the children collapsing,
limp spattered dolls in the
center of a village on fire.

Blessed are those who
do not hear cries cut short,
or gunshot or hooves,
who cannot feel lingering
grief. In the afternoon sun,
each rock flashes. In the wind,
each blade of grass is screaming.

Oronoco

Then, we showed settlers our ways to grow plants, and a fever came to
all of us: Virginia's alluvial bottomland greened — we cleared it all, even
hillsides, not for food crops but tobacco. Dark gold it was, and we gave
our land to it, built towns to trade it — it was like money, you could buy
provisions with it. We developed the dark-leaf, called Oronoco, harvested,
tied it in sheaves, sledded the heaped leaves down mountainsides, and
mules pulled the loaded wagons to Lynch's ferry. The leaves were cured,
stacked in hogshead casks, then poled downriver by black men in
bateaux. A gift to us, it seemed, this money and land enough for all, until
the earth itself failed us, its richness spent, and the topsoil drifted away.
We saw children hungry in a drought of our making, the plant a new
form of destruction. We went by moonlight to the fields, hacked stalks
down, held ceremonies, prayed, but greed spread like blight, and others
took the money, then the land. When tobacco went south, we planted
apple trees for them, became pickers of berries and fruit but were never
the same — we stood in the orchards at breaktime, smoked our ready-
rolls, coughing a little — we scuffed the ground with our feet when we
spoke and did not see each other's eyes.

Jamestown Revisited

after Wendy Rose

(upon being asked to attend a gathering at the site of the Jamestown
Colony, where church people intended to apologize to Virginia Indians
for everything since 1607)

Here you come again,
asking. Do you see
we have nothing
to give, we have given
like the ground, our
mountains rubbed bare
by hybrid black poisons
concocted from tobacco.

You would spread us on your
platform like graven images.
You could repent to us,
weep into your robes an
emotional, talk-show-like
moment to absolve almost
four hundred years, then
go home to mow your lawn.

You are not the ones
who burned our cornfields,
passed infected blankets,
treatied, pilfered, raped, or
traded rum. You are not
those who ask how can I help,
offer Indians your jobs,
or even vote to save the earth.

We are not the ones
whose children froze in rivers,
whose mothers wore bullets,
whose fathers left hearts
on this ground. We are not
those about whom was said,
They haven't the rights of dogs.

We are words of tongues
no one dared speak. We are
nameless, named by others:
mulattos and *mongrel*
Virginians. We are white flints
and chips of bone, pottery
sunk in red clay, black glass

like spearpoints found here,
of obsidian mined among tribes
who lived a thousand miles
west. We are refrains of our
grandparents' songs that drift on
night winds with our dreams.

You call us *remnants* now:
what remains of a fabric
when most of it is gone.
You have no memory —
we sank to our scarred
knees and said there was
nothing else to give.

You ask again, *Will we
come to your apology?*
A southeastern wind
answers you. Our ears
are not visible. Lips are not
visible . . .
O, we are the bones
of what you forget, of what
you thought were just lies . . .

Only our eyes look around.
Earth-toned eyes, forest
eyes, thunderhead eyes,
eyes flecked with gold, eyes
like obsidian, eyes that are
seeing right past you.

My Standard Response

I.

 The first question is always phrased this way:
 "So. How much Indian *are* you?"

II.

 We did not live in tepees.
 We did not braid our hair.
 We did not fringe our shirts.
 We did not wear war bonnets.
 We did not chase the buffalo.
 We did not carry shields.
 We were never Plains Indians.
 We tried to ride,
 but we kept falling off of our dogs.

III.

 A local official came to our office to ask our help with a city event. He had a splendid idea, he said. To kick off the event and show everyone in town that our tribe was still around, we should go up to the bluff over-looking the city and make a big smoke signal. Then they would know we were here.

 Who ever heard of smoke signals in the forests? I imagined us upon the bluff, lighting one of those firestarter bricks. We haven't made fire since the Boy Scouts took over. And how would the citizens know it was us? They'd probably call out the fire department.

IV.

 As they ask, they think, *yes,*
 I can see it in her face. High cheekbones
 (whatever those are) *and dark hair.*

 Here's a thought: don't we all have
 high cheekbones? If we didn't,
 our faces would cave in.

(But I do have a colonized nose.)

I'm sick of explaining myself.

"You know," I finally say,
"It doesn't matter to my people."
I ride off to my ranch-style home.
Time to weave a basket, or something.

Markings on Earth

At night when the streets of your cities and villages are silent and you think
them deserted, they will throng with the returning hosts that once filled
them and still love this beautiful land.
— *Chief Seattle*

Ten thousand years of history, and we find the remains
of ancestors removed from their burial mound, where stones
sank into the welcoming grasses and would
have stayed, sentinels over a shrine to the spirits
entombed there, but the river changed course. It did not save
these bones — it was lifting them out of the earth.

Nine hundred years before us, fifty generations, the earth-
diggers, Monacans, knew the land and buried what remained
of their families in thirteen known mounds. The dead were safe
where they lay, until, at an appointed time, we lifted stones
and carried our relatives to sacred ground. Releasing their spirits
required four nights of music and fire, the dark wood

charred into ash. We reburied them by a dogwood
grove, our mound rising, fifteen feet of earth
and Monacan bones. Encompassed in mist, its spirits
lifted toward the sky. Of the mound, what now remains
but a small hump, plowed down, the ceremonial stones
thrown away? So little is left us — nothing really, save

those few who listen with their blood, who might save
our people. Scientists, sifting through dirt for the scars of wood
postholes, tell us how to reconstruct our homes. Stone
axes, chipped flints, potsherds: we locate our markings on earth.
As the only descendants of a nation, we remain
to find ancestors stored in warehouses, bagged, labeled, their spirits

neglected, dust pressing over their bones in the spirit
of historical research. We are left among ruins to save
what we can, our grandparents who did not depart but remain
among us, as we may remain after nine hundred years. We would
bring them home, give their bones to the cradle of earth,
their songs and ours quivering through the stone.

We are their families, weeping for stones
we cannot find, for the blue shroud of spirit
rising like breath, for the tattered earth
we recognize but have not been able to save,
remembering stones, rivers, hills, dogwoods,
spirits. We are safe, for now. The earth and sky remain.

Moving the Mountains

I.

This you inherited: black-necked geese rising as one
up the flyway, calling to each other over walnut
and beech trees, over blue mountains to darken
the sky into gold and black filigree, gold in the grass.
Hills blaze through autumn, streams flash like mica,
brown-speckled trout break the surface at dawn.
These are always before you: dark cider, burning wood,
pork in the smokehouse, singing of fiddles. This, too:
a land come alive below the snow-crusted summit,
past gentian and laurel, across a lime-green valley floor,
tiny white churches, enameled barn roofs, cedar trees,
cows like a spatter of inkspots, layers of blue mountains
fading back into the sky. This, as your grandparents were,
is what you are, indentured to the land, into which
you too will go — the love you will make with your bones.

II.

It is not about faith. Remember strip mining, flanks
of the mountains gashed deep, the dirt? A marvel,
this cleverness: how draglines bigger than churches loom
like scaffolds with steeple-frames cockeyed, swivel
almost gracefully, shriek, then scoop building-sized
chunks of the mountaintop up, dumping them onto a valley
below. How this obliterates thousands of years, the work
of a man's hands, and trees, blossoms, streams, with one arc.
Remember the waste dam collapsing in '72, when sludge
and water bore down the hollow at Buffalo Creek. Water,
a 20-foot wall. Towns swept away. Litter of bodies.
The land, streaked for years. Now the foothill town
trembles from the blasts, dust rising to obscure it.
Again, boxcars glitter with coal mounds, the raw power
of earth, and here is that love at the root of everything.

III.

Orange haze hangs in the air after blasting. Flyrock,
in pieces the size of a child's head, screams through
abandoned backyards. Something is wrong with the water.
Small dark birds cower in the corners of your eyes.
Mountains are turned inside out, seen as gray ulcers
from space. Outside the barbershop old men slump
with the laughter gone out of their faces. One holds
a list: the names of families moved away, their houses
sold to the mines, bulldozed without reclamation.
When mountains and rivers end, what can remain?
Cairns become reliquaries, grass a stunned fuzz above rock.
On the bluff at sunset, a man guards his family's graves.
Silence settles over the rest of his life. You, on your knees,
look beyond the mines toward ridges lovely as Canaan
and the sky blooms, its glory relentless, behind you.

hard times

Hard Times

for Diane Shields

A woman sits on a porch of weathered boards,
her skin the color and texture of the dried-apple dolls
that grandmothers gave to children years ago.
When asked about the past, she will not speak.
They were hard times.

Maybe she sits on the parched earth instead,
looks toward fields of rice, cotton, sugarcane, tobacco.
Maybe she wears a printed housedress or sarong
with hair covered or plaited, her face etched
in memories of joy snatched from her
in daylight and auctioned to strangers.

Her hands have scrubbed cities of floors, washed
the nameless dead, cooked food for armies, so little of it
hers; hands that failed to protect her or any of her children.
She believes that if she speaks, she might break apart,
the dust of her flying across stooped men
chained by their debt to the fields. She presses both lips
together, an effort to hold her own grief in her skin.

Maybe evening wears into night. The stars that connect us
gather like sisters around her. We hear, *They were hard times,*
across the continuous land of our women, until as sun
rises above droning flies and the garrulous chickens,
a voice speaks in our old language, which we do not know.
We sift through a history with dust on our hands,
the empty rocker creaking in the breeze.

Colors

My mother found me in the
basement, seven years old with new
watercolors, painting my arms
Indian red because I couldn't
wait for summer.
     The school bus would
stop for the light
colored children and pass the darker
ones by. I remember a boy told
to move his desk out to the hall,
who tried to join Cub Scouts, but the
group was "too full."
     I think of
my daughters' pale, perfect
skin, lighter than mine, the way
their hair curls. They haven't painted
themselves yet, but in Aberdeen,
Seattle, Syracuse, or Richmond, a seven-
year-old with black hair or blonde will be
scrubbing or painting her hands or just
waiting for summer.
     And I say
let her be a moonflower
unfolding to the night. Let him be
Carolina's blue-shadowed black waters.
Let their children be
every shade of the soil that feeds us.

The Room

The drab olive bedspread was
patterned with soldiers who marched
where he sat, his hands flat,
as he said he was leaving.

While rain trailed rivulets down
the window, I pressed my cheek
to glass and saw him fade. My father
has hunched himself into a mouse,
a gray bug, a dot on the landscape
so many times. A vanishing man:
it is always surreal, how he goes.

My face is still hard against the glass.
Fifteen years gone — I am still
in a bedroom, watching little men
follow him out. They step
from my room as I sleep, hands
feeling for walls. I hear rain
through the windows; feet
march, echo back, and are gone,
they are — he is gone, a battalion
of small soldiers, leaving.

Four Weeks in July

Crisp stubs of grass
bristle underfoot.
In the fields, cornstalks
curl into curved backbones.
Leaves drop from trees.
We cannot find words
to pull water from the sky.

The dry hush of wind
blows dust into our mouths, open
as if waiting,
and into our eyes.

A bank of clouds sweeps in overhead.
Horses' ears prick forward,
Herefords lift their heads, katydids stop
their harsh rasping a moment.
From far off, a first roll of thunder
descends,
and the earth seems to shiver as
hairs on our bodies
rise.

Something Is Always Taking Us Away

in memory of M.P., 1962 – 1985

by moonlight, leaving no evidence
       A two-lane road, named for someone forgotten
(not a mark on you, they said)
       it is not dangerous. We know
from laughter, gathering upward
       we traveled this way every night
like smoke in an Indian car, no drivers swerving
       as workers cut through the crushed door
to rearrange roads, no bayonets aimed at our people
       their machinery burned against chilled air
when telephones work, while a lamp
       twisted into your seat, your face
shines, and there is no disease in the blankets
       still as snow on the windshield
no alcohol, no succession of suicides
       you could not see an ordinary truck
too soon, something taking us
       wedged within brush, watching you
gently, without the earth's tremor
       through headlamps. Nothing warned you
no roaring of cannon, when death is
       not the darkness, not the wipers, only
a patch of ice on a back-country road
       a truck driver's face, frozen, surprised.

Urban Nightmare

for Peter Klappert

All day we run gasping
Our scarred arms flail
We are talking long distance
to think ourselves safe   that sharp
rap   the pane shatters

They bang on our doors   they are
coming to burn our village

When we snatch the phone to scream
an operator drones
                    what city please

and we cannot remember names

Our lips split open
as we string wire between cities
lost to our own voices

Fire and Water

For years I have watched your
deliberate death, the precise way
your fingers clasped bottles
until small flames within them
licked your brain's capillaries,
searing each delicate fiber.
Wounded, you stalked my sleep,
pissed blood and bellowed until
you passed out, a ragged snore
reverberating back from every wall.
How you say I don't love you
because I could leave the way
a drowning person leaves water's
grip to stumble up the beach
clutching air. I left carrying
your voice, your scent about me
all the time, a thick smell of yeast
and decay, as though a cloud of you
had passed by. Remember, I would
have given my life to save you
the slow decomposition of all that
you were, could still be, how I stood
helpless, my empty hands
gloves that held nothing. I wake,
even now, in a palpable silence
to feel my bones chilled through
their sockets, this fear for you
burning like ice into everything I touch.

For My Ex-Husband

It begins slowly and small, like an incinerator's
fire, as it must, because no woman would
love what you became. After five years,
you would wake me in the night to interrogate
with candles, burning incense as your serum.
Whom had I seen, and when, did I
have lunch with any man? until, exhausted,
I began to understand why people may confess
to crimes. You and your psychologist —
Delusional, he said — you called it driven
mad with love. I left you anyway.
That night a year later, near Halloween,
you broke into my home and beat the man
asleep next to me until he had no face —
he left his cheek's pulp in his place as he ran
out, naked and faceless, and drove himself
away from both of us. You chose to rape me then,
dragged me by my ankles through blood and
shards of glass. Even today, I do not understand
how any man could do it or why you left me
alive, your own face contorted into nothing I
recognized; how, within minutes, you swept my
dignity, my god, the whole order of the world
as I knew it, away, how I remained imprisoned
in my own body as though it had stayed there
on the floor. After your incarceration, you visited
our child and wondered why I would not let you
kiss me good-bye. Because my skin would not
allow it. By day I cowered behind my own shoulders —
at night I dreamed of bullets. Finally, years after,

your mind let me go, but I did not believe it —
I stood squinting in the blue air as one among
the bony women who walked out of Dachau
wondering what I should do with the
shreds of woman left through every long
day that would follow, now that I could choose.

Confession Beneath Plum Trees

The air: enflamed throat of August. Dusk spreads
riotous membranes at field's edge, beneath the arbor.
As my vigil becomes heat, cicadas tune up —
am I surprised, nearing forty, by landscape intense
as my life still on fire — *I want, I want,* rasp of cicada.
This is the world, its darkening plain, white-fenced
as ribbon strips bind a gift awkward to hold —
in this scene, why introduce regret? Walking through
Georgetown summers ago, past a gate wrought
with a pattern of orderly vines, what if I'd taken
his hand, kissed or uttered a phrase? Who was
betrayed? In my palm, the hot plum colored like a bruise
could be any woman's heart. It tells the whole story.

Smoke

Those August nights, we sat by your workbench
in the garage and chain-smoked cigarettes,
smoke clenching upward, hovering, its stench
blown outside. We talked beside cords, fish nets,
wiring, hinges, clamps and cracked pails.
On a wall behind us, you'd traced the outlines
of hammers and staple guns, around nails
where they were meant to hang. At times
you'd found tools gone, while working on a flower
bed or deck, lost in piled leaves, their shapes
empty like chalked figures after a crime. Hours
of talk hurt us both — should I leave, try to stay,
which furniture belonged to whom — through all
this, those vestiges there on the wall.

In Memory of Shame

because it was our fault and because we did nothing wrong
because we spoke and because we had nothing to say
because we were ignorant and because we knew too much
because we neglected our children and because we wanted to protect them
because we drank and because we stopped drinking
because we were industrious and because we had no energy
because we were young, old, fat, bony, spineless, cocky,
      selfish, selfless, frigid, immoral, guilty

    because we loved too much or not enough
    because we couldn't fry an egg correctly
    because the house hid dust in its corners
    because we stayed and because we left
    because our faces were the wrong ones
    because we were treated disrespectfully
    because we were children or women or not
        white or just not enough.

Refuge

We left behind the shriek
of bright machinery gutting forests we knew.
In our own land, in English,
the word *refugee,* then *exile,*
where they teach other countries
how to make their people vanish.
We see persecution in the shadows of trees,
as a woman's severed hands are folded into a little box
and shipped to Washington for fingerprints,
or as some of us — burned, beaten, raped —
there is nothing that has not been done.

One night, over coffee,
your eyes were night's ice,
enflamed, like collapsing stars, eyes in a photo
of a man who disappeared. I whispered
through the continent's purposeful silence,
Give me papers. A name.
In São Paulo, Chiapas, Quebec, I become
another woman's native face
searching for eyes she has loved,
hair and skin she has loved —
I send poems across a landscape
dark as Kentucky, speak the name
that was yours, tuck your hands' memories
into my coat, wet with continuous rain.

On the trains, across borders
of sculpted barbed wire,
I hear the loud Americans
who speak of human rights,

how their government protects.
I wonder where they live,
where on earth their sanctuary is.

Amends

after Adrienne Rich

A morning like this: through the lace of the treeline
a new sun, its radiance
thrusting the elegant fingers of god
through the air: white light glints on curved tendrils

as it glints on stouter branches, as it swells across the river
clearing the beach with a sweep of its arm
as it splits the cliff's shadow, as it races up the hillside
as it sprints over the creeks

as it relentlessly gathers in the slashes
of the mine shafts
as, behind it, twisting fragments
scatter haphazardly

> *in a village, a woman lifts her hand*
> *looks at the sky, looks*
> *at the sky*

as it streams through the tent flaps into canvas shelters
that quiver with awakening
as it lingers, reflected in the eyes of those
who lie clothed in light now
       as if to make amends.

For Them

America, you ode for reality!
Give back the people you took.
—*Robert Creeley*

Where are they, then, who
vanished after breakfast,
walked through lavender-
scented streets in town, bought
nothing, brought nothing home?
who disappeared in daylight,
their belongings vague
shapes in unoccupied rooms?

The trees know. Wind-wracked,
they huddle together, women
wrapped in somber black shawls.
Here is a cry you have heard
through your life, your voice the air
over a field of human bones,
now the city's reflection as jagged
stairs spread out over the harbor.

They are around in a stirring
from elsewhere, the top foot
of earth, every bit of it, theirs.
You shape their absence.
Diminished by memory toward
your last days, you wonder where
they were taken, what they
might have known at the end.

first light

Endless Land

Flying west, over the plain of my relatives' homes,
my bones turn with knowings no one told me —
I can hear our songs buried under dry riverbeds,
past petroglyphs on mesas where the plane
touches down and the Rio Grande bends itself
to flow through this city where a Southeastern woman,
Cherokee or Creek, trips over heavy ground and falls,
face-down drunk, and tilts her head back
to the daze of half-being.
                              We meet with our eyes, the flicker
blood demands, and remember a journey of footprints
dragged west across the Appalachian snow, how we walk
backward with faces turned home, west across the river
where plains give themselves to new mountains
and a place speaks to us, and I say

I have seen rivers rage over dams to flood across the land
that could not help itself —
                              it cannot help us, sister,
but we could rise, too —
                              to know the true circle of voices
that call to us over this ground
                              open-mouthed in the snow,
voices of mothers and fathers who ask us
to hear the earth,
                              singing.

Veterans' Dance with My Father

We who dance apart
know well how not to say
what was abandoned
or migrated from
lost as our very bones
sink toward the past
history shoveled over
an inscrutable future.

As a boy no one told you
after pestilence   burning
slavery   massacres   turning the
people against one another
after the colonized rum-induced
shame of it   there were
no schools for us and we were called mongrels
so who could have told us
we survived?

We did, though   so dance
until your footpads feel drumbeats
Dance your haircut and denims
your tennis shoes   athletic socks
Dance the skin you called white
which is copper   Dance earth-
colored eyes, yourself in air-
force uniform forty years ago.
Dance the ancestors' voices
a heart that remembers
your relations   all of us
who have identified you.

Discovery

for Belle Waring

Picture my reflection profiled
in glass at the Fredericksburg bookstore. Outside,
the sun. I find your name on a book
like another scarred trinket
given up by the sea.
                    How, on a shining beach
twelve years ago, we dreamed of impossible men —
a sailor who later did time for assaulting his wife,
a Latin American somewhere in Paris, who, even now,
may be sifting cold ashes for cigarette butts.

Our old poems smolder like badly built fires.
When I think of you, it is not your face or your name
but a burn-through of images seen as yellow
linotypes,
                    skewed and out of focus.
You would have understood, me
crying in a bookstore, after
                                        such men.
I bought the book, Belle, and walked
into the sun to read your poems,
standing by my car, as though looking
for words to say how we survived.

The Lilies

When I learned I might have cancer,
I bought fifteen white lilies. Easter was gone:
the trumpets were wilted, plants crooked with roots
bound in pots. I dug them into the garden,
knowing they would not bloom for another year.
All summer, the stalks stood like ramshackle posts
while I waited for results. By autumn, the stalks
had flopped down. More biopsies, laser incisions,
the cancer in my tongue a sprawling mass. Outside,
the earth remained bare, rhizomes shrunken
below the frost line. Spring shoots appeared
in bright green skins, and lilies bloomed
in July, their waxed trumpets pure white,
dusting gold pollen to the ground.
                                                    This year,
tripled in number, they are popping up again. I wait,
a ceremony, for the lilies to open, for the serpentine length
of the garden to bloom in the shape of my tongue's scar,
a white path with one end leading into brilliant air,
the other down the throat's canyon, black
and unforgiving. I try to imagine
what could grow in such darkness. I am waiting
for the lilies to open.

The Bed

Though the carpenter   carefully copies
detailed drawings,   drives his chisel
true every time,   trims and sands

dovetails, dowels,   adds dentiled edge,
carves sockets,   spindles, shells,
bevels and burls,   the bed he toils

to finish, while pleasing,   is imperfectly planned —
according to Socrates,   whose Creator decreed
an ideal for each thing,   even an ethereal bed.

A holy bed —   how would it be heavenly?
In mere design,   or through masterful making?
Should it be scalloped   with sculpted scrolls

worked in wood,   walnut or ebony,
inlaid with ivory   or iridescent gems,
its velvet canopy   divinely violet,

with shimmering sheets   of shirred silk
that gleam in the dark?   Would we dare drape
limbs across its loveliness   or lie there after love?

Or, would the Maker   demand more —
a bed of blue   gentian, bordered
with pillows of pansy   and plump grass —

or a forest of ferns,   an efflorescent
field — the ideal   itself, imagined
without human help,   and hence holy?

We cannot find   perfection's favor.
Our bed bulges   in spots, and our bones
warp, grow porous,   weaken and wobble.

I would chip creases   from hollowed cheeks,
gently fill in   the fragile fingers,
scrape sagging   ruts from your skin,

mold you in marble   like Michelangelo
to keep us from the cold   unkindnesses of love,
which waits for us   to watch it go away.

Back to the bed —   if we could believe
in the sanctity of common   stained sheets,
pocked pillows,   unevenly puffed,

a thinning coverlet,   two troughs
tunneled in the mattress   by our time together —
we'd lie down,   make love until light broke

and rise, reconceived,   immortally radiant,
to leave our shadows   asleep as on silk,
each apparition aging   in the other's arms.

The Beginning of Fire

After the reading, as his fire cooled to ordinary air
and he shrank to the height of a man and his resonant voice
dimmed itself, writers gathered as though to pluck
words from his shoulders. One of them
asked a student to drive the poet to his hotel.

Unspoken, a ceremony centuries old, the young
woman offered by men of the village to honor a visitor.
Though he asked her to "come up and talk" (he was
probably fifty or older), she knew little
of language or fire and could not
find words. He was tired, he said. She turned to go,
stopped —
        What is her story? If she said
their clothes burned off in layers, that her skin
pressed toward his and awakened the warrior
within him, that fires escaped from their
opened mouths, sank as red coals through the mattress,
caught the hotel; if they walked out of that
orange glory, arms interlocked as though they were
the first people; if they never
looked back, what would he write then,
or how would his words taste to her,
those exquisite poems she once, only, licked from his tongue,
would it be different?
        Yes, she loved him —
not as one she knew, but as that original woman must have
loved the one who first brought her fire.
As the tongue of creation flicked across every warm thing

through history, flames began to resemble a hunger
that requires only memory to be born fifteen years
from any moment after its beginning.

Cactus Song

In the Valley of the Sun, heat thrums in white
waves as succulents contract, ribbed stems
and spines needing moisture. Your voice
inhabits my hotel room, the air, the tiny bones
inside my ears. Two thousand miles from home

in desert exile, I feel dry to the touch, dry as clay
in the fire pit, as blue cactaceous skin, my voice
a splinter of one who has not spoken in years.
Parched for you, my wanting almost makes you
visible, reassembling you from memory alone.

Today an elder from Tohono O'odham sings
with his rattle a song that urges corn kernels to grow.
This is how we retain what is precious, the love
of a thousand years, as a people's memory of rain
calls each delicate shoot through the sand.

Now he sings for fruits of saguaro and cereus,
draws buds to the surface, their fleshy scales
tipped burgundy and green, flowers tucked inside
like swans. I wonder if love forms nubs of those buds,
the way I am a cactus that holds you as water.

Smoke Dancers

Darkness stretches itself through winter months as a penetrating
cold into fur through elkhide and beargrease, entering skin
until it quivers in Haudenosaunee hands. The smoke dancers
step into the light, their singer tapping his water drum, its skin
the deer whose death blessed it into song. Cook fires wink
across palisaded towns, mirrors of the stars themselves.
The men dance quick steps to the beat—thighs like haunches
churning. They know their music, hopping
                                        mid-song at drum's pause,
then faster until smoke rises. It is done this way, though longhouses
are fewer. Men step toward the circle, begin as though nothing has
changed, as though men of their time, as they are. Now they dance
in a white tent—the audience leans forward, knows them as men,
and they pivot and stomp, leap and whirl, kin to the animals, they rise
as birds, sway as saplings, grow fluid like water, swirl and flow
as they become the air their people breathe.

Making Apple Butter

In late September, evenings bring Monacan women to the tribal center
kitchen, where they make apple butter. They gather their aprons,
headscarves tied on, descending the hillsides with dusk. The first night,
they pare, core, and quarter cooking apples, imperfect yellow spheres
stacked in bushel baskets — no crimson, waxed Delicious, no green
Granny Smiths, no Empires. All evening, women chop as apple chunks
turn the color of earth in the air, as leaves begin to yellow in the dark-
ness. They need one quart of apples for every half pint; baskets empty as
fingers grow moist, then wrinkle, among laughter and the scrapes of
small knives that pare and pare again.

The second night, boiling begins. Scents of hot cider, cinnamon, ginger,
and cloves rise to spread around the women like thick, hooded robes.
Quarts of cider or vinegar are stirred and stirred again, the hours it takes
to reduce each pot by half, to add the chopped apples, simmer an hour,
add sugar, spices, boil again, until dark-gold mixtures turn the mahogany
velvet of trees and the scent anoints the hair. Now, through the music of
spoons, jars, and pots, through laughter, what remains is reduced to the
essence of apple: roots and limbs laden with gold circles. We are blessed
by the hands of these women who ladle into jars an enchantment made
by heart, who condense, seal, process, and sell apple butter at St. Paul's
church bazaar, three dollars for a pint.

Order

In square bricked beds, tea roses and peonies bloom.
Her porch wears a shadow of thick Boston fern,
symmetrical in its basket. The polished kitchen, origin
of scents — baked apples, floor wax — is itself her home.

A red horse trots beside the fence. Barn tools hang
according to the season of their use, and in her arbor, cleft
scions of plum take root within each meticulous graft.
Between arbor and barn, two heaps of steaming dung

decay into compost. *Order,* she says, but in sleep her mind
carries her past fields toward the dark cathedral of trees —
she wants to run, deep in, beneath an arching canopy
as wilderness surrounds her, its order of another kind.

Red Hawk Woman

in memory of Thomasina Jordan

Now you are among us and now gone the way light
diffuses through forest and only remembers the sun.

Now you are red sky woman who sets fires to paint the clouds.
Now you are white breath woman rising through mountains at dawn.

Now you are yellow pollen woman who gives birth to blossoming plants.
Now you are black night woman with eyes that grow round in the dark.

We have seen death in its gracious and varied shapes all this time.
We saw battles where the best of us fell, and we cried for ourselves.

You rekindled in us a wisdom that flows with the blood, courage
to leave the grief we recalled for the grief we cannot yet imagine.

You led us into Washington, that city of bones, where we spoke
with earnest words the dreams our ancestors wished into us.

Now we give you back to the green skin of earth and here
lay down the quarrels and obsessions that weaken us all.

Now we take up your life in our hands and walk together,
our prayers the simplest act of remembrance.

O, Native woman wearing the songs of ten thousand
years in your hair, who among us is like you?

Walk with us through the darkness where we arm ourselves,
knowing it was not dying you taught us to do.

Before Your Mother's Death

As she sleeps, her shape diminishes.
Her face pales

and cools beneath our hands, beyond time or forgiveness.
Within soft folds of the brain,

the tumor branches out, a cauliflower.
Glioblastoma — the word like a bomb.

And we stand here separately —
we, who shared a bed, now stand as though

in different rooms. I wear your transgressions
like a rosary, naming every act,

but as I watch your mother sleep, her skin
ridged yellow, like a shell,

I see her as one who has renounced almost everything,
in whom our past unravels.

Her life begins
to break up. Within me, a shattering

like stone.
I cannot say the comforting words

or know what form
my language may find for itself,

but as we bend toward her, as the body
goes on, mostly out of habit, I discover

what remains to be said,
and I recognize you.

Between Us

I can hardly imagine myself within you,
turning, like a planet, within you,
the slow queue of silver-lined cells bunched up
to become individual hairs, fingernails,
teeth like stars, barely envisioned.

I can hardly imagine myself without you,
distinct and motherless, inevitable as it is
that I will be there on some ordinary blue evening,
as you were, with your mother.
I will hand you back to the darkness,
touch you, then turn away
as we do, to stumble
through a greater emptiness.

Among the unsaid things,
this is why we are content to sit
as twilight gathers
at the city's farthest edge,
to talk through various, inconsequential moments
and to laugh,
the butter softening,
the bread cooling on the table between us.

Another Visit to the Cancer Specialist

Darkness: the night gods
send your own terror to you —
owls on black branches.

Morning entrances.
The sky turns Pendleton blue —
everyday grandeur.

And you, old gambler,
fresh from the doctor's white room —
still beating the odds.

The Milking

"When I was nine," he began, and years flipped backward
until he was again a boy in overalls, milking at dawn.
Their only cow, dry on one teat two days in a row.
His father looked perplexed as though he wasn't sure
already and told him to wait up that night in the barn,
just to see. So there he was at midnight with a lantern,
in the scent of fresh-baled hay, among the murmurs
of horses and the workings of a hundred common spiders,
until his eyes bleared. But he saw it. A snake, maybe four
feet long, rose straight up like a black exclamation beneath
the cow's udder, milked with its head as though born to do it,
and the cow never moved. Then it vanished with no sound
at all. He walked to the house in a pathway of moonlight,
under the stars of that darkness in which
he might still believe almost anything actually possible.

The Man in the Road

Cresting a hill on Route 29,
tired from the drive, the sun strobe through trees' shadows
cast in diagonal bars, I saw
a man standing in the road; I mean, in the grass of the median,
waving, not just any old wave —
say, the half-hearted swipe of neighbors or barely perceptible
twitch to the postman —
this guy threw everything into it, his arm a dark rod,
fingers splayed
into the signal of glorious welcome, his whole face a grin.
Of course I waved back.
Every week since, I've driven that road, forgetting again,
until I'm near the place,
his broad teeth, the chestnut of his face below his cap, the arm,
upright. He'll be there
unless it's raining. The griefs of his past, whatever they are,
have not embittered him —
everyone who drives by receives his salutation. I don't know
why he does it,
whether he has little to do or knows that when he's gone he'll be
missed by more people
than most. Today I think of stopping — more likely I won't.
I'll just drive on,
waving like crazy, like he does. We will not discuss politics
or tragic histories.
It will never matter that we are not the same. What we are
to each other is nothing
more than a man in the road, a face that blurs by and our arms,
this brief recognition.

Returning

after Derek Walcott

You never forget: a white chapel, perched by the roadside,
the bulk of granite outcrop on which it sits like a hat,
the redbuds, yellowed now, the dogwood rusting, dignified
as a matriarch, as fluted leaves begin to encircle it,
the mountains against orange clouds to the west,
a chimney steaming with the season's first drift of smoke,
pale against the sky and sinuous as a woman undressed
in someone's window. Across fields, you hear the shriek
of a hawk, gliding over Bear Mountain, past spines of corn
arcing back toward the earth, and smell a faint reek
of apples shriveled together in the grass. The creek's bliss
continues under the road, behind trees, where a cabin
settles into the ground. *Can you genuinely claim these,
and do they reclaim you?* Dusty yards, red-rimmed eyes of men
in overalls, women with stained hands, their faces resigned
beyond the years, irreversibly, and are they your own? Their thin
voices, brittle as their joints; shelves in their root cellars, lined
with callused potatoes and onion bulbs, apples in barrels, rows
of home-canned provisions that gleam in jars; their cordwood
stacked in readiness, quilts on their beds. The autumn glows
around you, hilltops enflamed in the sun's last light. The land,
the land you never forget, rises, falls, and rises again, always:
yes, they reclaim you in a way you need not understand.

First Light

At this hour, who could discern where land ends,
or water, where creek becomes bay, bay becomes
river and stretches across to a blue verge
of Maryland, all the way black now, invisible.

Through July's haze, the first light is a brushstroke
of gray seeping in. Ducks totter up the beach,
short bowlegged sailors. Over the water, duck blinds
loom as improbable creatures who graze a pale field.

From the marina around the bend, two crabbers set out.
Their diesel chugs reverberate as prows cut new waves.
Mockingbirds swoop, flash their shoulders like women
advertising summer dresses. Herons cast themselves down.

What matters? At the end, we become what we have
loved, each thing that transfixed us in the rapture
of its moment, its grace of its own making, ours the same.
We grow around the land as it grew around us, and

dawn crosses over us, whether asleep in nests or
berths or in the ground becoming life again. Here is
the moment: here, among herons, ospreys, morning,
river. I believe in *this* light: it is the light of the world.

acknowledgments

I thank the editors of the following publications, in which most of these poems first appeared, often in different versions: *The American Indian Culture and Research Journal, The American Indian Quarterly, Black Bear Review, Black Buzzard Review, The Chattahoochee Review, The Chiron Review, Gatherings IX: The En'owkin Journal of First North American Peoples, Iris: A Journal About Women, Monacan News, Phoebe,* and *Potato Eyes.*

"Directions" and "Blue Mountains" appeared in *The People Who Stayed Behind,* Geary Hobson & Janet McAdams, eds. (forthcoming).

"Spider Dance" appeared in *Orion,* vol. 19, no. 2 (Spring 2000), p. 61. "Markings on Earth" appeared as originally titled in *Red Ink,* vol. 6, no. 2 (Spring 1998), pp. 61-62, and was subsequently published in *News from Indian Country* in late November 1998, p. 14A, with the title "Poem for Monacan Reburial." "In Memory of Shame" and "Red Hawk Woman" will appear in *Sister Nations,* an anthology of Native American women's writing, edited by Heid Erdrich and Laure Tohe, to be published by New Rivers Press, Minneapolis, Minnesota, in 2002. "Endless Land" appeared in *Feeding the Ancient Fires: A Collection of Writings by North Carolina Indians,* Marijo Moore, ed., The Crossroads Press, North Carolina Humanities Council, 1999.

Epigraphs and selected lines of poetry used verbatim or adapted are also gratefully acknowledged. The first epigraph by Joy Harjo is from "The Dawn Appears with Butterflies," which was published in *The Woman Who Fell from the Sky,* and is used with permission from W. W. Norton & Company, Inc. Lines 1 and 2 in the poem "Directions" pay homage to N. Scott Momaday. The epigraph for "Blue Mountains" appeared in a poem of the same title in *To Us, All Flowers Are Roses* by Lorna Goodison and is used courtesy of the University of Illinois Press, Urbana.

In the poem "Amoroleck's Words," the epigraph is from *Red Clay: Poems and Stories* by Linda Hogan and is used with permission from Greenfield Review Press. The last five lines of the poem are from John Smith's *General Historie of Virginia, Book 3.* Amoroleck was the first Indian of the Monacan confederacy to speak with the Englishmen from Jamestown and was captured by them near present-day Fredericksburg, Virginia, in 1608.

In "Jamestown Revisited," the fourth stanza, line 7, is from Bertha Wailes, "Backward Virginians," an unpublished Master's thesis, University of Virginia, 1928; the fifth stanza, lines 4 and 5 are from Arthur H. Estabrook and Ivan E. McDougle, *Mongrel Virginians* (Baltimore: The Williams & Wilkins Co., 1926); and the eighth stanza, lines 7 through 8, are from Wendy Rose, *Going to War with All My Relations,* used by permission of the author.

The epigraph in "Markings on Earth" is attributed to Chief Seattle, from the *Port Elliott Treaty,* 1855. The epigraph by Robert Creeley in "For Them" is from *Collected Poems of Robert Creeley, 1945–1975,* and is used by permission of the University of California Press.

"The Lilies" is dedicated to Dr. George Kaugars, Dr. Robert Strauss, and Dr. Laurence Dinardo of the Medical College of Virginia, with profound gratitude.

In the poem "Returning," lines 13 and 14 and line 23 are excerpts from "Christmas Eve," *The Bounty,* by Derek Walcott, copyright © 1997 by Derek Walcott, and are reprinted by permission of Farrar, Straus and Giroux, LLC.

I am grateful to George Mason University, the R.G. Bryant Monacan Indian Scholarship Fund, and the Virginia Council on Indians for fellowships that enabled me to complete these poems.

Special thanks go to Dan Becker, Dennis Campbell, Sam Cook, Curt Fontaine, Marijo Moore, Diane Johns Shields, and Micky Sickles, and to my many teachers.

about the author

Karenne Wood is an enrolled member of the Monacan Indian Nation and serves on the Tribal Council. She has worked as an editorial assistant, real estate agent, domestic violence victims' advocate, and as an activist for the rights of women and American Indians and for environmental issues. She has studied at the University of Virginia and at George Mason University and was a finalist for the Ruth Lilly Poetry Fellowship in 2000. She lives in Maryland with her family.